RAILWAYS
of the
YORKSHIRE DALES

Compiled by
MICHAEL BLAKEMORE

GREAT NORTHERN

In the same series:
RAILWAYS OF THE NORTH YORK MOORS

Great Northern Books
PO Box 213, Ilkley, LS29 9WS

This edition 2005
First published by Atlantic Publishers 2001

ISBN 1 905080 03 4

© Michael Blakemore, 2005

Design and layout: BARNABUS DESIGN & REPRO, TRURO

Printed by THE AMADEUS PRESS LTD., BRADFORD

British Cataloguing in Publication Data
A catalogue for this book is available from the British Library

CONTENTS

The 'Cream Special' at Northallerton on 26th April 1927. Dairymen propel the four-wheel trolley carrying milk churns and cream cans from the Wensleydale Pure Milk Society bottling plant for return to the Dales stations. A red flag on a pole denotes its presence instead of the more usual front and tail lamps! (NRM/Household collection 327)

⚜ INTRODUCTION ⚞

Mention 'Yorkshire' and the word 'Dales' often springs immediately to mind to accompany it – the two seem to go together. Yet it would be wrong to think of the Yorkshire Dales as a single entity; they are more a family of constituent members, some large, some small and little-known, each with its own identity and geographical character. The Dales embrace a wide area lying between the Pennines and the Vale of York; on the eastern slopes of the Pennines rise the rivers which form the dales as they make their way, joining others, ultimately to the sea. To the south west Wharfedale stretches away from the industrial towns and cities of the West Riding and is in considerable contrast to the more northerly and easterly dales of the Wensley and the Swale where the scenery is less rugged, more agricultural.

Whilst large parts of the smaller dales have been undisturbed by the coming of railways, most of the larger dales were opened up to rail travel either by terminating branch lines or by cross-country routes connected to other lines at either end. Not all the Dales railways were meandering byways, for on both the western and eastern fringes of the area important main lines forged routes to the north and south. On the west that most renowned of main lines, the Midland Railway's Settle—Carlisle route, was built in the boldest of gestures to form an integral part of its line from London to Carlisle. Over to the east the Leeds Northern line from Leeds to Northallerton, via Harrogate and Ripon, carried a Pullman service to Scotland and the important expresses between Liverpool and Newcastle.

One of the longest Dales branches connected them at Northallerton and Hawes Junction, though serving no large population centres along the way. Others served towns of some size and importance such as Richmond and Ilkley or market towns like Pateley Bridge and Masham. Local people were taken to work, to market, to fairs and holidays, to war, while increasingly in later years visitors were brought into the Dales to explore what HRH The Prince of Wales has described as "one of the most treasured landscapes in Britain".

As with so many secondary railways, those of the Yorkshire Dales have not fared too well with the passing of time. The Grassington branch passenger service ceased in 1930, the Wensleydale and Pateley Bridge branches followed during the 1950s and the sweeping cuts of the 1960s further took their toll, including the main line through Ripon.

But all is not gloom, by any means. The Settle–Carlisle line, for so much of the 1980s neglected and threatened with closure, was reprieved and is now enjoying a revival in fortunes, with recent refurbishment of track having been undertaken; its cheery stations and increased traffic are the positive indications of how a railway can be turned round. Another encouraging development during the 1990s was the electrification of the routes from Leeds and Bradford to Skipton and Ilkley; new trains are being introduced and the frequent services appear to be well patronised. Over in Wensleydale, campaigners have restored train services from Leeming Bar through Bedale and to Leyburn and onto Redmire on a line that survived to carry freight for almost forty years after its closure to passengers.

The full story of the Yorkshire Dales railways has been told expertly and in detail elsewhere. This book seeks only to provide a pictorial survey of the railway scene in this favourite part of the White Rose county – past and recent. My thanks are particularly due to David Beeken, John Edgington and Gavin Morrison for their help with photographs and to all those others – sometimes unknown – whose cameras recorded the views we now offer.

MICHAEL BLAKEMORE

WHARFEDALE

Wharfedale takes Yorkshire from the urban and industrial areas of Leeds and Bradford to the moors above Ilkley, Otley and Skipton. Heading north through either extemity of Wharfedale were two main lines — the Midland Railway's line from Leeds to Skipton and the Leeds & Thirsk (later the Leeds Northern then the North Eastern) route through Harrogate. Proposals for a line to connect them were put forward during the 'Railway Mania', the most notable being the Lancashire & Yorkshire North Eastern Railway which saw itself running from Skipton to Wetherby and York. Nothing of substance arose from this, even after the section east of a junction with the Leeds & Thirsk at Arthington had been abandoned by agreement with the latter. Subsequently the Leeds Northern arranged with private operators to provide 'omnibus' connections from Ilkley and Otley to Arthington.

The lack of mineral resources in Wharfedale had not inspired transport developments in the area and since nothing had come of various other abortive schemes, in 1859 local parties made approaches to both the Midland and the North Eastern which had hitherto been hostile to independent companies penetrating their territories. The result was that they agreed for once to work together to build a line through Wharfedale. The NER would build a line from Arthington to Otley, from there to Ilkley would be a joint undertaking, then the MR would provide a link from its route at Apperley to a double-ended junction at Burley. The Otley—Arthington section was opened on 1st February 1865, the rest of the route following on 1st August.

The railway was soon stimulating a population growth in places such as Ilkley and Otley; it even spurred the development of Ilkey as a health resort after the water had been found to contain sulphur efficacious in the treating of certain skin diseases.

Further additions to the Wharfedale railway network were inevitable. Firstly, in 1876 the MR opened a link from Shipley to Esholt Junction, south of Guiseley, which gave a direct route for trains from Bradford to Otley and Ilkley and on through to Harrogate. Given the growing popularity of the area of Wharfedale around Bolton Abbey, an extension of the railway from Ilkley to Skipton was a further logical move and this was achieved by the Midland on 1st October 1888. Bolton Abbey soon became a popular destination for excursions, while a range of through trains travelled via the Otley route, notably an interwar service between Bradford and Newcastle.

The cuts of the 'Beeching Axe' did not miss Wharfedale and the Arthington—Ilkley—Skipton route was closed on 22nd March 1965. Ilkley, however, remained rail-served by the line from Apperley Junction and the Shipley—Guiseley branch; moreover, they survived to see electrification in the 1990s! The Aire Valley electrification scheme was completed in 1995 and took in the Leeds—Skipton route together with the branches to Bradford Forster Square and Ilkley. A frequent service of electric trains now plies between these places and it is encouraging to see them well patronised.

A belated railway arrival in Wharfedale was the Grassington branch. Its origins, though, lay in grandiose schemes in the 1840s to create a new through route between Lancashire and the North East. The Liverpool, Manchester & Newcastle upon Tyne Railway of 1846 got nowhere, nor did other propsals in the 1860s and 1880s, then in 1895 the Yorkshire Dales Railway proposed a line from Embsay and Hellifield through upper Wharfedale and Coverdale to Darlington. This was far too ambitious a scheme for such a late date, so the company settled for an initial branch from Embsay to Grassington whilst doubtless harbouring thoughts of future extension.

The branch was opened on 29th July 1902 and was worked from the outset by the Midland, though the Yorkshire Dales Railway retained its nominal independence until the Grouping. Grassington remained the terminus; it was, in fact, named Grassington & Threshfield since it was situated mid-way between the two. Such an inconvenient location no doubt contributed to a lack of patronage and the branch passenger service fell by the wayside as early as 22nd September 1930. Grassington nevertheless remained a favourite destination for excursions, particularly for ramblers, and a goods service continued until 11th August 1969. That, however, was still not the end of the Grassington branch as a large limestone works at Swinden continues to generate traffic to this day.

Finally, mention must be made of the fact that the name Yorkshire Dales Railway lives on in the form of a preservation society based at Embsay which in 1979 re-opened a short stretch of the Skipton–Ilkley line. Although not the biggest or most famous of preserved railways, it extended its track to give a round steam-hauled trip of three miles and in 1998 opened a further extension to Bolton Abbey where it built a splendid re-creation of the Midland Railway station.

A busy moment at Otley's sizeable station in Edwardian days. A North Eastern Railway Harrogate train is on the left, while the rear of a Midland train can be glimpsed on the right.

An LNER train on the Midland route from Apperley Junction — D20 4-4-0 No.2393 heads a Leeds—Ilkley express through Menston on 11th June 1947. (H.C. Casserley)

The ubiquitous North Eastern Railway G5 0-4-4Ts could be seen on the Leeds—Ilkley via Arthington trains. An unidentified specimen is pictured in the woods near Ben Rhydding c1950. (G.T.G. Findley)

The terminal platforms at Ilkley during the 1930s — Midland 2P 4-4-0 No.562 awaits departure running tender-first probably to Bradford.

The Aire Valley electrification in 1995 was a bold step forward but no new rolling stock was provided to herald the new age. Instead Class 308 electric multiple units, built in 1961 for the London, Tilbury & Southend lines but made redundant there, were transferred north for a further lease of life. Here is a pair of three-car sets at Ilkley on 31st August 1995. Note the Midland Railway quarter-mile post on the station wall, denoting 211¼ miles from St. Pancras.
(T.J. Edgington)

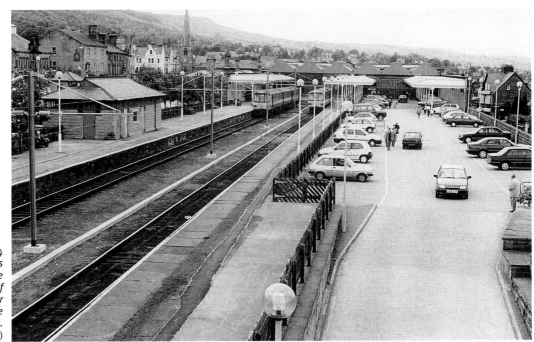

Ilkley station on 28th May 1994 with 'Pacer' diesel units for Leeds (left) and Bradford Forster Square (right). Occupying the trackbed of the former through lines is a car park but a pleasing touch is the retention of the platform canopies.
(T.J. Edgington)

Ilkley station consisted of two terminal platforms (the original Otley & Ilkley Joint Line terminus) and two through platforms for trains on the Midland route to Skipton. LMS 'Patriot' 4-6-0 No.45505 The Royal Army Ordnance Corps heads out of Ilkley towards Skipton with a return excursion to Whaley Bridge on 15th May 1955. Following closure of the Skipton route the bridge over the road has been removed.

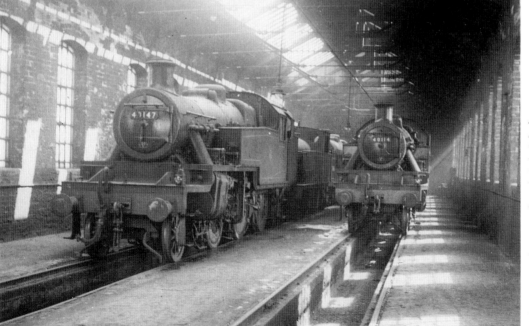

A joint MR/NER engine shed was provided at Ilkley in 1866, originally close to the station where it was subject to complaints about smoke nuisance. With the opening of the Skipton line, the opportunity was taken to move the depot to a new site north of the station in 1892. Engines were outstationed from Leeds (Neville Hill) and Bradford (Manningham). As a sub-shed of Manningham, Ilkley depot closed on 5th January 1959 when diesel units took over local services. Resident on 22nd April 1956 were two Stanier LMS 2-6-2Ts Nos.40147 and 40114 and an ex-LYR 2-4-2T No.50636. (F.W. Smith)

In LMS days Lancashire & Yorkshire Railway 2-4-2 radial tanks infiltrated Wharfedale and examples could be found shedded at Manningham and Ilkley into BR days. Here is No.10880 on a local at Bolton Abbey.

Embsay Junction, with the Midland Railway signal box positioned between the Grassington branch diverging to the left and the main line to Bolton Abbey and Ilkley.

Limestone has been despatched from Swinden Quarry, near Rylstone, since the opening of the Grassington branch. Latterly, steam motive power was provided by BR Class 4 4-6-0s from Skipton and then Carnforth depots. In a bare landscape awaiting the coming of spring, No.75026 makes its way towards Grassington with a freight, including coal hoppers, on 17th March 1967. (Gavin Morrison)

Ilkley station on 30th July 1966 and a Leeds train waits at Platform 3, one of the now abandoned through platforms. Note the portable steps to compensate for the low platform. (Colour-Rail)

A Skipton—Ilkley DMU (with the early yellow 'whiskers' which pre-dated yellow visibility panels) approaches Bolton Abbey station in August 1964. (Colour-Rail)

Grassington c1905, immaculate and still new-looking after its opening only three years earlier. The station seats have the full name 'Grassington and Threshfield' taking up their entire length!

A poignant photograph at Grassington station on 21st September 1914. Only six weeks into what was to be known as the 'Great War' and these young recruits, full of patriotism and optimism, have answered the call to arms and are off to join the colours. One wonders how many would return.....

Although the Grassington branch lost its passenger services in 1930, excursions — particularly ramblers' specials — continued to make occasional visits. LMS 4F 0-6-0 No.44041 prepares to leave with the empty stock of a ramblers' excursion from Bradford in April 1950. (David Joy collection)

Goods traffic to Grassington continued until 1969. Here is a 4F 0-6-0 shunting on a damp Dales day amid some fine signals; there are two Midland lower quadrants and a bracket in the distance, while an LMS or BR upper quadrant shunting arm has been installed on a MR yard signal post. (David Joy collection)

15

ABOVE: *An established feature of the preserved Yorkshire Dales Railway's motive power policy has been the use of industrial locomotives. Here at Embsay station in 1986 is a train double-headed by a pair of 0-6-0STs* Slough Estates No.3 *(built by Hudswell, Clarke & Co. in 1939) and NCB No.S134* Wheldale *(built by the Hunslet Engine Co. in 1944 for the War Department and later used at Primrose Hill Colliery, Swillington, and Wheldale Colliery, near Castleford).* (T.J. Edgington)

RIGHT: *The restored LNER K4 2-6-0 No.3442* The Great Marquess *heads 'The Dalesman' railtour between Otley and Burley-in-Wharfedale on 4th May 1963. On the right can be seen the Midland route via Menston and Guiseley to the Aire Valley main line.* (Derek Penney)

Since 1969 the limestone aggregates traffic has kept the remaining stretch of the Grassington branch open between Skipton and Rylstone. Between 1970 and 1973 Swinden Quarry (by then owned by Tilcon-Tilling Construction Services Ltd.) was modernised and expanded to double its output, with new hopper wagons constructed. On 30th July 1992 BR Class 60 No.60 095 Crib Goch rounds the curve to the site of the former Embsay Junction with the 10.16 Swinden—Hull train. (Gavin Morrison)

NIDDERDALE

To the east of Nidderdale passed a now-vanished main line — the Leeds Northern route from Harrogate through Ripon to Northallerton — along which expresses such as those running cross-country from Liverpool to Newcastle used to thunder. This originated as the Leeds & Thirsk Railway, authorised in 1845, and soon after construction started it had its eyes on extensions to the north via Northallerton and Yarm to join the Stockton & Hartlepool Railway. Parliamentary powers were sought but George Hudson exerted pressure to have the stretch between Melmerby and Northallerton dropped from the scheme so that trains would use his Great North of England Railway between Thirsk and Northallerton.

The railway was opened between Ripon and Thirsk on 31st May 1848; Weeton to Wormald Green was ready for opening on 1st September 1848, followed by the intermediate link from Wormald Green to Ripon on 13th September. Opening of the route down to Leeds awaited the completion of the 3,791yds-long Bramhope Tunnel and the entire line was not open throughout until 9th July 1849.

The Leeds & Thirsk had very soon looked again at extending north from Melmerby to Northallerton and obtained powers to do so in 1848. In 1851 the company changed its name to the Leeds Northern Railway and its main line became an important through route. However, by the 1960s British Railways was no longer regarding it as essential and services north of Harrogate were withdrawn on 6th March 1967.

Leading off the Leeds Northern a delightful branch line penetrated into Nidderdale itself. The possibility of a branch to Pateley Bridge had been raised by the Leeds & Thirsk but after obtaining Parliamentary authority it allowed the powers to lapse. It was left to the North Eastern Railway to revive the proposal and the branch from a junction at Nidd, just north of Harrogate, was opened on 1st May 1862.

The Pateley Bridge branch (14½ miles from Harrogate) made its contribution to life in the dale until competition from motor buses proved too great and it became an early British Railways closure victim. Passenger services were withdrawn on 2nd April 1951, though goods traffic continued until 31st October 1964.

Pateley Bridge was, however, by no means the end of railway penetration into Nidderdale; further up the dale was a source of perhaps even greater railway interest. To provide further reliable water supplies for its growing city, Bradford Corporation at the end of the nineteenth century was planning to construct reservoirs in Nidderdale; the first, the Gouthwaite Compensation Reservoir, was completed in 1901. In that year a Light Railway Order had been granted for a 2ft 6in gauge line from Pateley Bridge to Lofthouse to open up the northern extremity of Nidderdale. When by 1904 nothing had been done about it, Bradford Corporation decided to take over powers for the line to use in connection with its next programme of reservoir building. Construction of the Nidd Valley Light Railway began in July 1904 when a civic party from Bradford travelled on the 3ft works railway already existing between Lofthouse and Angram. This was extended to Pateley Bridge that year but in May the Board of Trade had agreed to its conversion to standard gauge. This was undertaken in 1906/7 which then enabled wagonloads of construction material to be worked through from the NER.

Bradford Corporation had also acquired an obligation to provide a passenger service between Pateley Bridge and Lofthouse, a distance of 6¼ miles, and this was formally inaugurated on 11th September 1907. The line beyond Lofthouse was used only to convey men and materials for the construction of the reservoirs. After eleven years the Angram reservoir was finished but it was another five years before work started on the next, Scar House.

The NVLR's passenger service did not last long — just over 22 years. It was discontinued from 1st January 1930, though goods traffic continued to the Scar House reservoir site. Soon after the reservoir had been completed in 1936, the railway was closed and dismantled.

On 30th May 1967 LMS 'Jubilee' 4-6-0 No.45562 Alberta
was unexpectedly used to head a Royal Train, conveying
the Duke of Edinburgh, from York to Nidd Bridge. After the
Duke had alighted, No.45562 took the train forward to
Ripon in order to run round and is seen at Wormald Green,
three months after the line had closed to passengers. This
was the last steam-hauled Royal Train. (Gavin Morrison)

LEFT: *Another view of the surprise 'Jubilee' - hauled Royal Train working on 30th May 1967. No.45562* Alberta *has run round the stock at Ripon before returning to York.* (Gavin Morrison)

BELOW: *The photographer has recorded a rather special 'cop' at Ripon in May 1935 in the distinctive shape of the unique Class W1 ' Hush-Hush' 4-6-4 No.10000, fitted with water tube boiler, on the 4.17pm Newcastle—Liverpool. This experimental locomotive had just returned to service after modifications at Darlington Works to fit a Kylchap exhaust and was working from Leeds Neville Hill shed on expresses to Newcastle.* (J.W. Hague/D.V. Beeken collection)

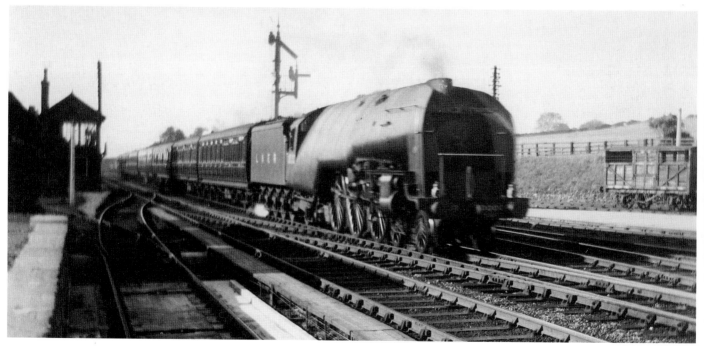

Another reminder of when main line expresses between Leeds and the North East used the Leeds Northern line through Ripon. A4 Pacific No.4494 Osprey is seen heading north, wearing the standard apple green livery it carried from new in August 1937 to October 1938 when it was repainted garter blue. A further change in 1942 saw it renamed Andrew K. McCosh. (J.W. Hague/D.V. Beeken collection)

Nidderdale Agricultural Show

Mon 22nd Sept

Cheap Day Tickets

will be issued to Pateley Bridge at ordinary single fare for the return journey from all stations within a radius of 60 miles

Available any train

FOR CONDITIONS OF ISSUE SEE OTHER SIDE.

Tickets, bills and all particulars can be obtained at the Stations, also at the usual Town Offices. For further information apply to the District Passenger Managers at Leeds (Tel. No. 20615) and York (Tel. No. 2264).

TICKETS CAN BE OBTAINED IN ADVANCE

London & North Eastern Railway

LEEDS Sept 1930   1712—Petty & Sons (Leeds) Ltd—7,000

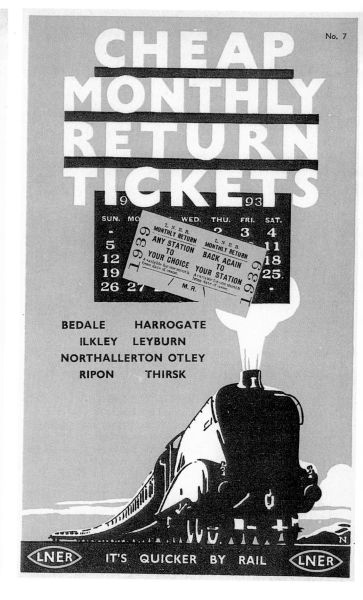

A 1930 handbill for cheap travel on the Pateley Bridge branch.

The LNER had a flair for publicity and made good use of stylistic representations of its A4 streamliners and the 1937 'Coronation' streamlined train. Passengers beginning their journeys at some of these Dales stations would not, however, find anything quite so exotic awaiting them! (D. V. Beeken collection)

The NER's Class Z Atlantics were fine-looking machines and as LNER Class C7 here is No.710 leaving Ripon with a down pre-war express.
(J.W. Hague/D.V. Beeken collection)

*A North Eastern Railway Class R 4-4-0 — LNER Class D20 — No.2384 calls at
Ripon with an up local service cNovember 1948.* (J.W. Hague/D.V. Beeken collection)

A3 No.60086 Gainsborough *races south through Melmerby in the early 1950s. On the left the Masham branch curves away, the platform fenced off following its closure to passengers some twenty years previously.*
(J.W. Hague/D.V. Beeken collection)

*The 'Queen of Scots' Pullman (King's Cross—
Leeds—Edinburgh—Glasgow) was the prestige
train on the Leeds Northern route. On 12th July
1950 A3 No.60084* Trigo *was in charge of the up
train passing Middleton Lane, Melmerby.*
(J.W. Hague/D.V. Beeken collection)

Hurrying through the hayfields at Monkton Moor, A3 No.60081
Shotover has the assistance of D20 4-4-0 No.62378 (which has
sustained a scorched smokebox door) on a Newcastle to
Liverpool express during the early 1950s.
(J.W. Hague/D.V. Beeken collection)

Pateley Bridge station on 8th April 1950 finds G5 0-4-4T No.67284 just arrived on the 1.35pm from Harrogate. The glazed conservatory-type structure was an unusual feature of this branch terminus. (T.J. Edgington)

No.67284 again on the same train as in the previous picture, this time blowing off steam at Dacre as it waits for passengers to unload themselves and their belongings. This was the busiest intermediate station on the branch, handling timber, agricultural produce and high-grade sand.

Seen at Lofthouse on the Nidd Valley Light Railway is the Kerr, Stuart steam railmotor built for the Great Western Railway in 1905 and bought by Bradford Corporation in 1921. It was named Hill *in honour of Sir James Hill, a long-serving member of the waterworks committee and Lord Mayor of Bradford in 1908/9.*

4-4-0T Holdsworth *was acquired for use on the NVLR in 1906. Built by Beyer, Peacock & Co. in 1866, it was previously Metropolitan Railway No.20. It is seen outside the NER roundhouse at York, as repainted by the Metropolitan at Neasen, on its way to its new home. The engine is named after Alderman W. Holdsworth, chairman of the waterworks committee.*

0-6-0T Milner *was built new for the Nidd Valley by Hudswell, Clarke & Co. in 1909 and was used on the passenger service until replaced by the railmotor in 1921. It then moved to Scar Village for passenger and goods work and was sold in 1934. It took the name of an earlier* Milner, *the other of the pair of Metropolitan 4-4-0Ts which was sold in 1914.*

Blythe *(an Avonside Engine Co. 0-6-0ST built in 1922) and the railmotor are seen outside the two-road shed at Pateley Bridge. The water tank is a delightful Heath Robinson affair, seeming to consist of every bit of construction material around!* (Photomatic)

Lofthouse station en fête *on 11th September 1907 for the opening of the Nidd Valley Light Railway by the Lord Mayor of Bradford. Pateley Bridge is away in the right-hand direction.*

Pictured in 1928, 0-4-0ST Craven, *supplied to Bradford Corporation by Hudswell, Clarke in 1920, amid some of the huge stone blocks hewn from the surrounding hillside for the construction of the Scar House dam.* (Photomatic)

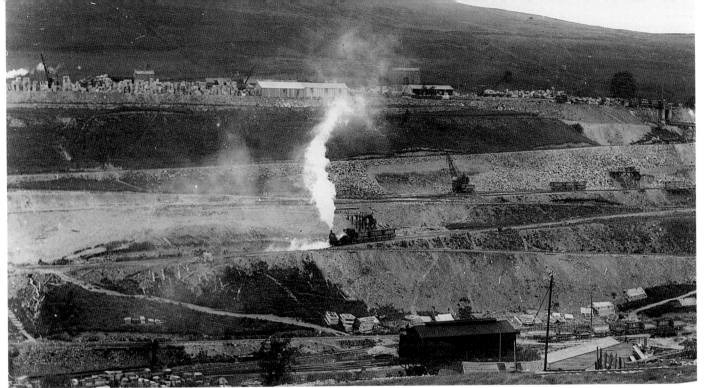

The Scar House reservoir construction site. The stone was mostly quarried locally and the railway brought in huge quantities of cement. Construction began on 5th October 1921; the cost of the project was £2.5 million and the reservoir — 1,054ft above sea level and covering 172 acres — has a capacity of 2,200 million gallons. Overlooking the site is Scar Village containing residential hostels, school, shops, mission church, concert hall, dining rooms and bathrooms. (Photomatic)

A freight for the Scar construction site in 1928 climbs the bank above Lofthouse with Milner in the lead double-heading with Blythe; another pair of locomotives is banking at the rear. (Photomatic)

THE MASHAM BRANCH

An Act of Parliament was obtained in 1871 by the North Eastern Railway for a branch just over seven miles long from Melmerby, north of Ripon on the former Leeds Northern main line, to Masham, a small market town on the River Ure. The actual terminus was in Burton-upon-Ure, about ½-mile outside the town and on the opposite bank of the river. Construction of the branch began in 1873 and it opened for traffic on 9th June 1875.

Reservoir construction also played a part in the history of the Masham branch. In 1901 Harrogate Corporation gained authority to build Roundhill Reservoir, some five miles south west of Masham. A construction depot was established at Leighton to which materials were carried by road from Masham station, but damage was soon being caused to the roads. A railway had been established from the Leighton depot to the site of the dam and in 1904 Harrogate Corporation was empowered to extend its line into Masham where the NER provided a transhipment siding from its goods yard.

Once the Roundhill reservoir had been completed in 1910, the works railway was taken over by Leeds Corporation which was building the adjacent Leighton reservoir. The outbreak of war in 1914 put that project into abeyance and the site huts were taken over firstly for military accommodation and then to hold German prisoners-of-war. The Leighton Reservoir was eventually completed in the 1920s, following which the line was abandoned.

As for the Masham branch itself, it became an early victim of a lack of passenger traffic when trains were withdrawn from 1st January 1931. Goods traffic continued to run and there was a considerable upturn in traffic during World War II when the area around Tanfield was chosen as a storage point for ammunition. The volume of munitions grew throughout the war until 76,000 tons were handled, while in the six weeks leading up to D-Day 42 ammunition trains were run.

The local pick-up goods struggled on until 1963 but it seems that by then trade was rather thin. In November 1962 the MP for Darlington complained in the House of Commons that the branch was being kept open just to supply fresh water to the crossing gatehouses and to deliver coal to Masham and Tanfield for sale by the Masham station master (this was a concession with the job going back to NER days). Whatever, time finally ran out for the Masham branch when the goods service was withdrawn on 11th November 1963.

LNER J39 0-6-0 No.64855 is caught in a rural setting overlooked by the village church at Tanfield as it crosses the Ripon to Masham road with a solitary mineral wagon for Masham on 4th March 1953. With such light traffic, it is perhaps surprising that the branch goods continued for another ten years. (J.W. Hague/D.V. Beeken collection)

NER A6 4-6-2T No.9791 trots away from Melmerby with two empty wagons on the Ripon—Masham goods on 4th May 1949. The main line towards Northallerton is in the background.
(J.W. Hague/D.V. Beeken collection)

The following day the same locomotive had a rather better load as it ran back down the branch towards the junction at Melmerby.
(J.W. Hague/D.V. Beeken collection)

An early photograph of Masham station in the 1880s with NER 2-4-0ST No.84 heading the branch train. Station and train do not seem to be short of staff! (NRM 6/01)

0-6-2T Leeds No.1 *was built by the Hunslet Engine Co. and supplied to Leeds Corporation in 1905 for the construction of the Leighton reservoir.*

RIBBLESDALE, DENTDALE AND GARSDALE

No book on the railways of the Yorkshire Dales would be complete without inclusion of the Settle to Carlisle line. It may not entirely fit in with the "Byways" concept of this series, yet for much of its life it has undoubtedly been a secondary route.

This spectacular railway over the Pennines has had a chequered career. Conceived in the late 1860s by the Midland Railway, desperate to have its own access to Scotland, it was almost killed at birth. Apprehensive of the costs of building a trunk route through such inhospitable country, the company patched up an agreement to gain access to Carlisle over the tracks of its old enemy the London & North Western Railway. But a Government fearful of monopolies threw out the abandonment Bill and the Midland was forced to proceed. It says much for the company – and the high ideals of the Victorian age – that it did not indulge in cheese-paring tactics. Instead it built the most magnificent of railways.

The Midland had good reason to be apprehensive. Constructing the line over rain-sodden uplands, once succinctly dismissed by a Dales farmer as "nowt but scenery", proved to be a heroic undertaking. Enormous shanty towns sprang up to house the navvies who for seven long years laboured with pick, shovel, wheelbarrow and precious little else. Construction costs were woefully underestimated and Midland shareholders grew anxious. There was no mood for elaborate ceremony when the line finally opened to passengers on 1st May 1876.

Once the Midland became part of the LMS in 1923, the glory days of the Settle to Carlisle were over. It was now a secondary route, useful for slow-moving freight traffic and the odd express on its way from St Pancras to Glasgow or Edinburgh. Years of decline appeared to be coming to an inevitable conclusion in 1983 when British Rail officially announced its intention to withdraw services.

The upshot was the most bitterly fought closure campaign in railway history. Objections were lodged by no fewer than 22,265 people – and one dog! Matters became highly political and dragged on for years, the line becoming such a focus of attention that passenger numbers increased from 93,000 in 1983 to almost half a million five years later. Finally, in 1989 the Minister of Transport announced a reprieve.

For the second time in Settle-Carlisle history, a railway company was now compelled to spend reluctant millions. Long neglect has been put right, viaducts repaired, stations improved, track renewed and signalling modernised. Heavy freight traffic has returned and the line now carries a more intensive local passenger service than at any time in its history.

The journey is memorable. From Settle the climb up Ribblesdale is on a ruling gradient of 1 in 100 – known to generations of perspiring firemen as the "Long Drag". This is the heart of Three Peaks country, with splendid views of Penyghent, Ingleborough and Whernside. The 1,000ft contour is crossed just before Ribblehead with its famous viaduct – 24 arches soaring over 100 feet above the surrounding moorland and yet utterly dwarfed by the nearby mountains.

The line curves gradually northwards to reach Blea Moor and what is arguably the most remote signal box in Britain. The black hole of 1 mile 869yd Blea Moor tunnel takes the traveller through to a very different landscape: a shelf high above the green floor of Dentdale. Dent station, highest on the line, is four miles distant from the village it purports to serve.

Another tunnel – 1,213yd Rise Hill – leads through to Garsdale, where were situated the highest water troughs in the world. Garsdale station, junction for the Hawes branch (see Wensleydale chapter), once boasted a small engine shed and a unique turntable stockaded as protection against the wind. Passengers becalmed by late-running trains could use a library in the waiting room, while railway staff had a social centre – complete with piano, stage and upholstered seats – beneath the huge water tank.

Garsdale is close to one of the great watersheds of northern England, where the rivers Ure and Eden rise within yards of one another. Here too is the line's 1,169ft summit, beyond which it leaves the rugged Yorkshire Dales and descends into the softer surroundings of the Eden Valley.

*A photograph that bears all the hallmarks of Eric Treacy, the 'railway bishop'
who portrayed Settle-Carlisle country in a way that few have equalled. The
setting is Skipton, southern gateway to the line. 2-6-4T No. 42492 is departing
with a local service on the branch to Colne, closed in 1970.*

HOLIDAY EXCURSION
TO
ESHTON HALL.

The Committee of the KEIGHLEY MECHANICS' INSTITUTION, beg to announce that they have made arrangements for an Excursion to Eshton Hall, the Residence of MATTHEW WILSON, Esq.

On Whit-Monday, May 28th, 1849.

THE PARTY,

ACCOMPANIED BY THE KEIGHLEY BAND,

Will leave the Railway Station at half-past Twelve o'clock and proceed to Skipton, at which place a number of BOATS will be in readiness to convey them to Eshton Hall. After spending the Afternoon in visiting the

SPLENDID GROUNDS
&c. &c.

connected with that place, which, through the kindness of MR. WILSON, will be thrown open, the Party will return to Skipton, which place they will leave at Eight o'clock.

The Members and Friends, headed by the Band, will leave the Mechanics' Institution in Procession, at Twelve o'clock precisely.

Tickets to Eshton Hall and back;—

First Class, 2s. 6d.—Second Class, 2s. Third Class, 1s. 6d.

May be had of Mr. Aked, Mr. Hudson, and Mr. Crabtree, Booksellers.

The Male and Female Classes will receive their Tickets at the Institution, on Thursday and Friday Evenings, from half-past Eight to half-past Nine.

Persons intending to join the Party, are requested to purchase their Tickets on or before Saturday Evening, that the Committee may make their arrangements accordingly.

J. L. CRABTREE, PRINTER, KEIGHLEY.

Visitors were flocking to the Yorkshire Dales well before the Settle-Carlisle line was conceived. The railway had been open to Skipton for little more than 18 months when Keighley Mechanics' Institution arranged this grand Whit Monday excursion – complete with band. Passengers simply walked across the road to the Leeds & Liverpool Canal, from where narrow boats would take them to Gargrave and the "splendid grounds" of Eshton Hall.

Bell Busk, one of the attractive half-timbered stations on the "little" North Western Railway, opened in 1849 from Skipton to Ingleton. Here passengers for Scotland changed trains to continue their journey – an arrangement that was far from satisfactory and eventually drove the Midland to conceive its direct route from Settle to Carlisle. Bell Busk was for many years the station for Malhamdale, horse-drawn "conveyances" taking passengers to gaze in awe at Malham Cove and Gordale Scar. (David Joy collection)

Hellifield became an important junction station in 1880 with the opening of the Lancashire & Yorkshire line from Blackburn and Clitheroe. This line-up of locomotives alongside the coaling stage was photographed in October 1937.
(David Joy collection)

Hellifield, still with an air of bustle on a summer afternoon in 1960. 'Crab' No. 42833 from Kingmoor shed is heading a Carlisle-Stourton freight past North Junction signal box. Careful scrutiny reveals various Stanier locomotives clustered round the shed on the right. (John M. Hammond)

A 'Crab' 2-6-0 heading south enters the short Stainforth tunnel under the grounds of what is now a youth hostel. (D. Ibbotson)

Derby No. 9, one of the contractor's locomotives used during the building of the line. The location is believed to be Helwith Bridge. (Mary Farnell collection)

Settle-Carlisle country personified, with the unmistakable shape of 2,273ft Penyghent in the background. From this viewpoint the mountain has been likened to a crouching lion. Class 40 No.40 094 is crossing the river Ribble near Helwith Bridge with a northbound freight in May 1981. (Gavin Morrison)

Winter has always been a factor on the Settle-Carlisle, most notably in 1947 when the line was blocked for two months by deep snow. Severe problems returned early in 1963 when this Edinburgh-London sleeper train was engulfed by drifts south of Rise Hill Tunnel. A heroic rescue operation was necessary to get the passengers back to Carlisle.

The highest water troughs in the world were to be found on the remote stretch of line between Rise Hill Tunnel and Garsdale station. Keeping them free of ice in the winter months could be a near-impossible operation. 'Crab' No. 42819 is crossing with an up freight consisting mainly of tank wagons. (J.W. Armstrong Trust)

After years of what was officially described as 'wanton neglect', British Rail found itself facing a huge backlog of maintenance work when the line was reprieved in 1989. This took its most dramatic form with the closure of the route later that year so that work could go on day and night at Ribblehead Viaduct. In such a lonely location, the battery of arc lamps made an eerie sight. (R.W. Swallow)

9F 2-10-0 No. 92019, one of the class most closely associated with the line in the last years of steam, leaves Blea Moor Tunnel with the Long Meg gypsum train. Spoil heaps from the tunnel shafts can be seen on the distant moorland.
(A. Sainty collection/Colour-Rail BRM742)

New era on the Settle-Carlisle. A group of Raleigh International volunteers, building new car parks and fencing at Garsdale station, takes a break to watch Flying Scotsman *storm past on the Guild '92 Steam Special.* (Linda Viney)

Ais Gill Summit, 1,169ft above sea level, where the line leaves the Yorkshire Dales and enters the Eden Valley. A gypsy caravan is an intriguing item on this freight leaving the up refuge siding behind 4F No. 44451 in July 1961. (Derek Cross)

51

The afternoon stopping service from Bradford Forster Square to Carlisle came close to the once common concept of a mixed train. It often conveyed more vans than coaches and called at no fewer than 26 stations on a leisurely journey occupying almost four hours. Characteristic 5MT motive power was at the head of the train in August 1964 when it crossed Arten Gill viaduct, one of the most attractive structures on the line. (Roger Bastin)

The Settle-Carlisle now has a more intensive local passenger service than at any time in its history. Most of the workings are by 'Sprinter' units, as seen here in glorious weather in Dentdale. This view well shows the dry-stone walls that are such a feature of the railway – and have been extensively restored in recent years. (Pete Shaw Photography)

SWALEDALE

At the northern end of our region the market town of Richmond stands as a gateway to Swaledale. Further up the valley, and in neighbouring Arkengarthdale, lead was mined for hundreds of years, carried down by horses. With the coming of the railway age it was taken to railheads at Croft and Cowton on what was to be the East Coast Main Line but the provision of a rail connection into the dale was an obvious attraction to promoters.

In 1844 the Great North of England Railway applied for powers to construct a branch from Eryholme Junction (originally Dalton Junction), 5¼ miles south of Darlington, to Richmond. The Act was passed on 21st July 1845 and the 9½-mile branch was opened on 10th September 1846 by what had by then become the York & Newcastle Railway. Intermediate stations were established at Moulton, Scorton and Catterick Bridge.

At Richmond a handsome terminus with overall roof was provided to the design of the well-known York architect G.T. Andrews. The facilities included an engine shed, goods warehouse and small gasworks. The station was located on the opposite side of the Swale from the town, so the railway company built a bridge across the river to give access to it.

Various proposals were floated over the years to extend the line: to Reeth, Hawes and Settle in 1845, to Reeth in 1869, to Muker and Hawes in 1881. Absurdly ambitious schemes were suggested to use the branch as part of a Darlington to Hellifield route and even a link between Barrow-in-Furness and the east coast, but none saw light of day and Richmond remained as far as the railway penetrated into Swaledale.

Though the lead-mining industry declined, another source of passenger and freight traffic came to the Richmond branch with the opening of a large army camp at Catterick in 1915 and a military railway, with a total mileage of some five miles, was built to serve it. At the time of its establishment the Great War was at its height and up to 45,000 men were stationed at the camp at any one time, with some 750,000 passing through it in a year. The military railway acquired a motley assortment of former main line locomotives and stock, though these were disposed of after the end of the war. Catterick Camp was further developed during World War II. There was a passenger service (worked by the LNER) between Catterick Bridge and the Camp, some trains running through to Darlington. A feature of operations for many years was a service of trains in the early hours of Sunday and Monday mornings for soldiers returning from weekend leave.

An interesting signalling experiment took place on the branch in 1911. At this time various systems were being tried which would give an indication in locomotive cabs to the aspect of signals during fog. Vincent Raven, Chief Mechanical Engineer of the North Eastern Railway, devised a system of electrical cab signalling in which steel brushes on the locomotive came into contact with metal ramps between the tracks. When these ramps were energised they gave a continuous indication of the state of the signals. Only locomotives fitted with the necessary apparatus were permitted to work the branch. The system was taken out of use in the early 1920s but it can be counted as one of many steps along the way to the Advanced Warning System in use today and, indeed, the Automatic Train Protection envisaged for the future.

Whilst troop trains during the two world wars brought spells of intense activity to the branch, a memorable one-off busy day was on 29th June 1927. The Richmond branch shared with the Wensleydale line the distinction of being chosen by the LNER as a main destination for excursions for observers of the total eclipse of the sun taking place early that morning. Five specials came up to Richmond — two from King's Cross overnight (one including sleeping cars), one from Marylebone and Great Central main line stations, and one each from Edinburgh and King's Lynn. An additional shunting engine was allocated to the branch for the day, along with two service trains which followed the last special to provide water tanks and gas for the excursions stabled along the up line between Richmond and Catterick Bridge.

The Richmond branch was proposed for closure in the 'Beeching Report' but managed at first to stave off the axe. A reasonably busy service — eleven trains either way Monday to Friday plus an extra 'Saturday night out' working — continued to link Richmond and Darlington until 1969 when on 3rd March the economists finally had their way. Goods traffic continued to Catterick Bridge until the following February, after which the branch and camp line were lifted. Richmond station nevertheless continues to give service to the local population — after closure it was converted for use as a garden centre and a swimming pool was built on the site of the goods yard!

LNER A5 4-6-2T No.9830 at Catterick Bridge and about to cross the Great North Road with the 7.20pm Richmond—Darlington, led by some NER clerestory coaches, on 22nd June 1947. The A5 class was originally a Great Central Railway design introduced in 1911 for London area suburban services; when the LNER needed additional powerful tank engines for the North Eastern Area shortly after the Grouping, the GC design was adopted and a further thirteen built by Hawthorn, Leslie & Co. of Newcastle in 1925/6 of which No.9830 was the first. In February 1944 munitions being loaded in the station yard exploded, killing twelve people and injuring 102 and badly damaging the station buildings.

The army camp at Catterick was rail connected and generated a substantial volume of freight over the years. On 9th March 1966 LNER K1 2-6-0 No.62041 was working the pick-up goods in the camp sidings and easing over the ungated road crossing under the protection of a flagman, with the shunter riding on the rear steps of the tender. (J.S. Gilks)

LEFT: *The Richmond branch terminus in 1965. The station building was designed by G.T. Andrews and the roof covered three tracks but only one platform; the other platform was outside the roof to the right and culminated in a horse-loading dock.* (David Sutcliffe)

BELOW: *During a quiet moment at Richmond the train and station staff await custom in front of a large poster advertising the famous Newcastle Brown Ale. After closure the station was converted for use as a garden centre.* (David Sutcliffe)

Darlington shed's L1 2-6-4 tanks were used on Richmond branch services and No.67750 is departing with what appears to be a special carrying express headlamps.
(J.W. Hague/D.V. Beeken collection)

Wensleydale is a fertile valley with agricultural land bounding on to the River Ure and is noted for its dairy produce — not least its famous cheese. Running east to west through Wensleydale from the East Coast Main Line at Northallerton to the Midland Railway at Hawes Junction (later Garsdale), on the Settle—Carlisle route, was a branch line of some 39 miles built in a curiously piecemeal manner.

The first section took the form of a branch from Northallerton to Bedale, promoted in 1846 by the Newcastle & Darlington Junction Railway, part of the empire of George Hudson, the so-called 'Railway King' of York. At this time the NDJR was leasing the Great North of England Railway (which had built the York—Darlington main line) and soon obtained powers to purchase it. From 27th July 1846 the new company was known as the York & Newcastle Railway which a year later amalgamated with the Newcastle & Berwick company to form the York, Newcastle & Berwick Railway. All this took place while the Bedale branch was under construction but as part of the fall-out arising from the downfall of Hudson it was not fully completed, stopping short at Leeming Lane. It was the YNBR which opened this extent of the branch on 6th March 1848.

The next 11¾ miles to Leyburn were promoted by the Bedale & Leyburn Railway, which was also empowered to complete the remaining original stretch between Leeming Lane and Bedale. The YNBR subscribed to the construction of the line and undertook to work it on completion. The 'missing link' to Bedale was opened on 1st February 1855 but by then the amalgamation of the YNBR, the York & North Midland and the Leeds Northern had taken place which created the mighty North Eastern Railway. The Bedale—Leyburn section was opened to freight on 24th November 1855 and to passengers on 18th May 1856, then in 1859 the local company was formally taken over by the NER.

There were various further proposals to construct railways through Wensleydale as part of schemes for through routes and branches, none of which actually came to fruition. One which came nearer than others was the Hawes & Melmerby Railway Act, passed in 1865. The NER, driven by its desire to keep out competitors, offered to subscribe half the cost but economies forced postponement of the project and when it became necessary to renew its powers, the NER decided instead to go for just the cheaper option of an extension of the existing branch from Leyburn to Hawes. This was authorised in 1870, with the

sixteen miles being opened to goods on 1st June 1878 and to passengers four months later.

The final link in the chain came from the west. An 1866 Act of Parliament had given the Midland Railway authority to build its Settle—Carlisle main line and also provided for a 5½-mile branch from Hawes Junction to Hawes where it would meet the NER. The Settle—Carlisle opened in 1876 but it was another two years before the Hawes branch was ready; goods working began on 1st June 1878 and passenger services on 1st October, the same date as the NER's branch opened from Leyburn.

The NER gained running powers from the joint station at Hawes over the Midland down to Settle Junction but only exercised them in respect of passenger trains as far as Hawes Junction. The MR did not exercise its own running powers eastwards to Leyburn other than for occasional excursions.

The Wensleydale branch for the most part lived a quiet life. Passenger traffic in such a rural area was light; the LNER's winter 1934/5 timetable showed five trains on weekdays between Northallerton and Hawes, four of which ran through to what since 1932 had been known as Garsdale, with an afternoon LMS train between Garsdale and Hawes. On Tuesdays only there was an additional morning train from Garsdale to Hawes and back, this being Hawes market day. However, there were peaks in the form of excursion traffic, particularly from the industrial towns of the West Riding and to destinations such as Leeds or Scarborough from the dale's stations. The branch's busiest day, though, was undoubtedly 29th June 1927 when early in the morning a total eclipse of the sun occurred across northern England. Eight specials for eclipse-watchers descended on the Wensleydale branch from King's Cross and Grimsby, Normanton and Castleford, Nottingham Victoria, Scarborough, Leeds, Hull, Norwich and Colchester, and Dewsbury. The trains were stabled along the branch between Leyburn and Aysgarth. At Leyburn two catering trains consisting of a kitchen car and a pair of third class open carriages were positioned in the horse dock and goods siding to provide refreshments.

Milk traffic played an important part in the working of the Wensleydale branch — and not just milk, but also butter and the famous Wensleydale cheeses. In fact, in the 1900s the afternoon Midland goods was instructed "to wait till butter is ready on Tuesdays"! Early in the twentieth century local farmers formed a

Despite the closure of the Wensleydale branch to passengers in 1954, passenger trains continued to appear from time to time in the form of excursions. On 20th May 1967 the 'Three Dales Tour' visited Leyburn behind K1 2-6-0 No.62005 and BR Type 2 diesel No.D5160. (Colour-Rail)

co-operative — the Wensleydale Pure Milk Co. — and in 1905 took the rental of a bottling plant built by the NER at Northallerton. In 1932 milk vans were being despatched to Newcastle and Sunderland, West Hartlepool, Tynemouth, Hull, Dewsbury and London (Finsbury Park and Queen's Park). Mention must also be made of the 'Cream Special', a hand-propelled four-wheel trolley pushed from the dairy into Northallerton station conveying churns and cream cans for the dale's stations.

With the meagre pickings to be had from such a sparseley-populated area, it was no surprise when British Railways withdrew the passenger service between Northallerton and Hawes on 26th April 1954. One train either way continued to ply between Hawes and Garsdale until 16th March 1959 when the former Midland section closed completely, though Hawes continued to receive goods traffic from the Northallerton direction until 27th April 1964.

Stone traffic had been a feature of the Wensleydale branch's traffic since 1908. A number of sidings existed, one of the most important being west of Redmire for the Redmire Limestone Quarry Co., opened in 1920. After local goods traffic was progressively withdrawn from the village stations, traffic from the Redmire quarry kept the branch open until 18th December 1992. The Wensleydale Railway Association was formed to secure the reopening of the line, a fairy godmother appearing on the scene in the surprising form of the Ministry of Defence. It decided to invest money in the branch to make it suitable for conveying army vehicles to Redmire, close to the Catterick Garrison. The first train ran on 15th November 1993 and this sporadic traffic has continued to the present day. After many frustrating setbacks, the Association saw passenger services restored between Leeming Bar and Leyburn on 12th June 2003 and on to Redmire on 1st August 2004. Extension of services to Northallerton is a high priority, the position being complicated by the pending upgrade to the East Coast main line. At the other end of the line there are hopes of an early reinstatement of three miles of track to Aysgarth. This would not only convey visitors to the famous Falls but also open up the possibility of a halt platform close to Bolton Castle, where Mary, Queen of Scots, was once imprisoned.

A truly rural scene at Finghall Lane which possessed just a single platform and a crossing box. A single coach suffices for the passengers but J21 0-6-0 No.65038's minimal load is supplemented by a milk tanker. A tethered goat watches its passage in a break from keeping the banks well cropped. (N.E. Stead)

J21 0-6-0 No.65075 calls at Leeming Bar heading a mixed train from Northallerton with milk tankers at the front early in BR days; in the background is the Vale of Mowbray cooked meat factory, another source of local produce traffic. At the east end of the station the Great North Road crossed the railway by a level crossing.

Finghall Lane in NER days at a time when small rural stations were lavishly furnished with accommodation and staff who had plenty of time to attend to the horticulture!

The delightfully-named Constable Burton station receives a call from G5 0-4-4T No.67314. Village stations often have eccentric-sounding names but Yorkshire must be unique in having not only Constable Burton but also Burton Constable (on the Hull—Hornsea line)!

By far the busiest day in the life of Leyburn station was on 29th June 1927 when it was host to special excursions run for observers of the solar eclipse taking place early that morning. Here are crowds waiting to board one of the return trains. On the right are catering vehicles for the benefit of passengers and a gas tank for replenishing restaurant car kitchens. (H.C. Casserley)

Another view of the Wensleydale branch's busiest day. D20 4-4-0 No.711 and B16 4-6-0 No.1372 await departure from Leyburn with a return excursion after the eclipse on 29th June 1927 — more motive power and carriages than the branch service normally warranted! (H.C. Casserley)

LNER Class Y3 Sentinel shunter runs through Leyburn station with four milk tankers on 27th February 1954. (J.W. Armstrong Trust)

Redmire station in the 1900s with its staff standing guard over their immaculately-tended domain. The station master is presumably the character standing by the bay-windowed office. (NRM 327/86)

G5 0-4-4T No.67345 pulls away from Redmire in the early 1950s. The immediate railway infrastructure has changed little since North Eastern Railway days with a fine assortment of that company's slotted signals, but beyond the single platform can be seen the stone loading plant for a traffic which gave the branch a life into the 1990s. (J.W. Hague)

With stone traffic keeping the branch in business long after the passenger service had ceased, BR Class 37s Nos.37 517 and 37 514 pass the closed (but still tidy) Redmire station on 30th April 1990 with a train of loaded hoppers heading towards Northallerton. (Gavin Morrison)

*A new traffic for the Wensleydale branch in the 1990s was tanks for the Army,
Redmire being the nearest railhead to the training grounds of Catterick Camp.
On 14th February 1997 a couple of tanks await unloading at the new dock with
two BR Class 47s Nos.47 213 and 47 033 in attendance.* (Gavin Morrison)

A moment in time captured at Hawes on 19th September 1953. An LMS 2-6-2T is at the head of the 4.25pm to Hellifield and a young lady has been allowed to have a look in the cab!
(J.W. Hague/D.V. Beeken collection)

A main line flyer demoted to secondary duties, ex-NER D20 4-4-0 No.62347 drifts into Garsdale with a train off the Wensleydale branch in the early 1950s. The Midland main line up to Carlisle is to the left of the picture and the up home signal can just be seen to be off for a southbound train which will presumably connect with the Wensleydale local. Despite over 40 years of closure, the course of the branch to Hawes can still be clearly discerned by travellers on the Settle—Carlisle route.
(J.W. Armstrong Trust)

On the Midland section MR 4F 0-6-0 No.43893 (with tender cab) is working hard on the 1 in 50 gradient as it leaves Mossdale Head Tunnel with the 5.10pm Hawes—Skipton Class H freight on 21st April 1954.
(J.W. Hague/D.V. Beeken collection)

LEFT: *North Eastern Railway G5 0-4-4T No.67278 has its tank replenished at Garsdale on 20th February 1954 after arriving with the 9.50am from Northallerton. Originally known as Hawes Junction, Garsdale is some three miles from any sizeable settlement and was established as a junction rather than to serve any immediate population. The row of houses beyond the station is railway cottages.* (T.J. Edgington)

RIGHT: *A stone train makes its way down the Wensleydale branch between Redmire and Wensley behind a Class 60 on 28th February 1992. Bolton Castle is in the background.* (David V. Beeken)

BELOW: *The famous turntable at Garsdale with its stockade to prevent locomotives being caught by the strong winds which blow at this exposed location. D20 4-4-0 No.62388 takes a spin on 19th September 1953.* (J.W. Hague/D.V. Beeken collection)